PONDERING OVER POETRY - 2

A COLLECTION OF POETRIES AND QUOTES

KRISH KHESKANI

Contents

Contents

Contents

CONTENTS

CONTENTS

1. Rains

The clouds covered the sun,
Like a mother protecting her child,
The exhausting heat is prevented,
Winds are soothing and mild.
Gusty winds with an aeolian sound,
The raindrops kissing the ground,
The trees shaking due to breeze,
Harsh conditions, they face with ease.
Gale filled with an earthly scent,
Pitter -patter sound marking the event,
Warm soups, tea, and coffee,
Making rains so comfy.
Washes away soil impurities,
As well as human negativities,
A nature's hymn all can hear,
Calms the mind, overcomes fear.
Dry leaves turn green,
Thunders are heard and seen,
Near the puddles was a frog,
It jumped over the road's clog.
The cars splash rains on each side,
The traffic in puddles like a water ride,
The scenic beauty, a nature's delight,

Escalated with a rainbow's sight.
They are the sky's joyful tears,
Which it held for almost a year,
It is now a season to express,
Stop delaying, it's time to confess.
That feeling of tiny raindrops on skin,
Like a holy shower about to begin,
Body refreshed by a spiritual gale,
Rains are nature's fairy tale.
~Krish Kheskani

2. Flowers

Some of them droop,
Some of them bloom,
Portraying prosperity,
And dangerous doom.
The pretty petals,
Like different life levels,
Wither off smooth and slow,
As we level up and grow.
Like a flower, maintain gentle fragrance,
Of genuine human affection,
Like pretty butterflies,
Good things follow in life's section.
Yellow rose for friendship,
Red, they say is for love,
White is for purity,
Peaceful like a dove.
Sunflower bright and yellow,
Directing towards the sun,
Like God guiding us to good things,
Also identifying "the one".
Lotus with strength and purity,
Strongly seated in a pond,
Like a special person on your mind,

Sharing with you a loving bond.
-Krish Kheskani

3. We will get through(Covid)

Trains have stopped,
No planes are flying,
Due to an invisible virus,
Millions of humans dying.
Masks and gloves are added,
To our daily dress codes,
Melodious chirping of birds,
Swapped honking on roads.
Realised why on maid's leave,
Moms have a broken heart,
Lockdown has taught me,
Household chores are an art.
A single handshake,
Or a touch leads to spread,
How can one's silly sneeze?
Turn another person dead.
For the ones suffering,
I pray you'll be fine,
Don't panic and run away,
Save others by quarantine.
Don't trouble the heroic police,
Respect them and be kind,

The stupid ones beating them,
Need to sanitise their mind.
Pessimists do hear me out,
We're at our lowest pollution,
These days are surely tough,
But soon we'll find a solution.
Feel the birds are lucky,
To dominate the sky,
I envy every creature,
Free to walk and fly.
Use time to try new things,
Learn skills you never tried,
Do some chores or read books,
Keep the negative news aside.
This will surely end soon,
The earth is just healing,
I think "Home sweet home"
Is not many people's feeling.
We're in phase of uncertainty,
Amongst negativity and death,
Stop worrying about 'Kya hoga?",
Meditate feeling your breath.
Relentless efforts of doctors,
And blessings of the almighty,
We'll soon get through pestilence,
Though corona seems mighty,
We'll soon live freely again,

Shaking hands without anxiety.
~Krish Kheskani

4. Quarantine Mood

Just woke up rubbing my eyes,
Don't know the day or date,
Is it too early to wake up,
Or is this a bit late.
Is my meal a breakfast,
Or is this my lunch,
I wonder what is going on,
I'm daily having brunch.
When I say 'Good morning',
It's always almost noon,
I barely see the sun much,
I'm friends with stars and moon.
The day feels short,
And the night so long,
Life schedule is haywire,
Everything feels wrong.
Never thought stepping out,
Could be a dangerous task,
Sad but true, you might die,
If you take off just a mask.
In every few hours,
I think of another nap,
In my dream last time,

I saw Modi ji clap.
Feel the birds are lucky,
To dominate the sky,
I envy every creature,
Free to walk and fly.
Learning things at home,
That never thought to try,
Washing dishes, cutting fruits,
And how to bake and fry.
Just after having snacks,
I ponder what more to eat,
I had snacks six times today,
I "Eat, Sleep, Repeat".
I completed the series in a day,
Which earlier took a week,
I watch a movie daily,
Share memes and snap streak.
Many teens fallen in love,
Texting love to their valentine,
While I connect with old friends,
To share stories of quarantine.
Trapped in my house,
With internet, phones and food,
We are stuck but safe,
Feeling the quarantine mood.
~Krish Kheskani

5. See you soon

Time seems so slow,
Finally, I reached noon,
Hope you're doing fine,
Want to see you soon.
I miss your lovely voice,
Soothing as a croon,
I wanna feel your vibes,
Want to see you soon.
Wish I could feel your breath,
Maybe I sound like a goon,
Wanna hold your hand,
Just wanna see you soon.
I feel incomplete,
You're my night's moon,
I want you around,
Want to see you soon.
In these lonely days,
Your memories are a boon,
Wanna know you more,
Want to see you soon.
You're my other half,
We're like fork and spoon,
Done with video calls,

Want to see you soon.
We call this quarantine,
I feel stuck in a cocoon,
Wish I could fly away,
Just to see you soon.
I know your fav song,
My ears still hear its tune,
Tired of seeing your photos,
Want to see you soon.
I'm like the air of love,
Trapped in a balloon,
I miss you way too much,
Want to see you soon.
April has been awful,
Hope we meet before June,
Since the last good bye,
I want to see you soon.
~Krish Kheskani

6. Women are Warriors

They battle to give and take birth,
"Abort her!", the family screams,
The strong woman carrying another,
Rebels to live her motherly dreams.
As she takes her first breath,
The family wishes she were a boy,
Some evils leave her on a street,
As if she is a toy.
In her teenage she is taught,
Kitchen is where she belongs,
They can't dance, sing or study,
She is a victim of society's wrongs.
When she is in her youth,
She is restricted on how to dress,
For wearing a short skirt,
They tag her "shameless".
She decides what to wear,
Based on where she goes,
If she is with people unkown,
Or around ones she knows.
Men often abuse and beat her,
She can't go alone at night,
Some wicked men out there,

Have created this fright.
Parents always yell at daughters,
"Don't wear this, it's too short",
Instead, "Lessons of respect women",
Their sons must be taught.
Some say small clothes worn by her,
Is an invite to misbehave,
Such people with rapist ideology,
Shall be buried in a grave.
Some men creep her out,
By stalking her at every place,
Their ego can't accept a "no",
So they throw acid on her face.
She is soon forced to marry,
Her own home she leaves away,
Dowry gifts to get rid of her,
To ensure "What will people say".
Holds a baby for nine months,
Watches her health till it's birth,
She is blessed with power,
To bring life on earth.
She is called unclean,
Though it's normal to bleed,
The society adds to her pain,
This must change indeed.
You are born and nurtured by a woman,
Learn to respect even the other,

Remember just like yours,
She is someone's sister or mother.
The oppressive society criticise,
She is still brave enough to rise,
See her with respectful eyes,
Disregarding her clothes, colour or size.
You're strong and beautiful,
Seen by my eyes,
Ignore what society says,
They're just stupid lies.
~Krish Kheskani

7. Terrorism

"Come back soon",
The soldier's mother said,
But the next time they met,
She saw him lay dead.
Terrorism is atrocious,
I feel it's a shame,
You can't kill innocents,
In patriotism's name.
Civilians also suffer in anguish and die,
When public places are under attack,
Their families are horrified,
Realising they won't come back.
They went out for work or to relax,
All injured at least a leg or hand,
Some were taken to the hospital,
And some buried in sand.
Why can't these terrorists,
Talk about their problems instead,
They believe war is the only way,
As they have a brainwashed head.
To kill other people,
You have no right,
To defend themselves,

Nations are forced to fight.

Humans are worse than mice,

A mouse never sets a mouse trap,

In the desire for revenge,

People's behaviour turns crap.

~Krish Kheskani

8. Non-consensual touch

Be it your lover,
Or a childhood friend,
No one can touch you,
If it's a no from your end.
Non-consensual touching is brutal,
It's not seductive, it's assault!
The victims are forced to be quiet,
Though it's not their fault.
The victims should speak up,
Putting the culprits to shame,
Society needs to understand,
The victims are not to blame.
Stop saying "She was drunk",
Don't blame her short skirt,
The only thing to blame,
Are those minds full of dirt.
You own your body,
Carry it with pride and grace,
Bravely shout 'No',
On invasion of personal space.
Society teaches men to be dominant,
So they can't take a 'No',
It makes them more violent,

Triggering their ego.
Society needs to teach their sons,
To be gentle and kind,
Parents should have a "boy talk",
To control the urges in son's minds.
Men need to accept a 'No',
And learn to step aside,
Taking consent is important,
It doesn't affect your manly pride.
This problem is seriously ugly,
It's always been prevalent,
But this can end soon,
By knowing importance of consent.
~Krish Kheskani

9. Tale of a Bullied kid

Everyone has left him,
There is no one by his side,
Life seems like,
A roller coaster ride.
They made promises saying,
They'll always be there,
Now it feels that,
They just don't care.
Everyone excludes him,
They say it's his mistake,
For them, leaving him,
Was a piece of cake.
In the corner of the class,
How badly he cried,
Always getting ignored,
When talking to them he tried.
Everyone talking about him,
Asking questions and putting blame,
He was a tender cheerful soul,
Seeing him cry is a shame.
~Krish Kheskani

10. Classroom

As the first bell of the day rings,
For the prayers all rise,
Most of them just lip sync,
Trying to open their eyes.
The teacher shouts with rage,
"Say it loud and join your hands",
All chant for next few seconds,
The sitting last bencher now stands.
Now enters the class clown,
The one who is often late,
Made an excuse as always,
"Ma'am I slipped at the gate".
The teacher yells at all,
"The worst class I've seen",
While all of them exchanged smiles,
Feeling prouder than ever been.
"I will tell the teacher",
The scary words of a nerd,
All that you did and said,
This one saw and heard.
One boy found it fun,
To imitate teachers during lecture,
All end up smiling while speaking,

As they can't forget his picture.
There was an enthusiastic guy,
The sportiest in the town,
Came to school in a white shirt,
After lunch which turned brown.
A charming boy and sassy girl,
Who had been crushes for all,
"Out of the league" they're called,
For you, they'd never fall.
Another is a lover guy,
Who finds a two-way crush,
To see her face, often is in a rush,
As he hears her name,
He can't stop his blush.
The guy near the door,
Always saves the day,
Warns all to zip their lips,
When teacher is on the way.
The class gave hoots of joy,
When teacher cancelled the test,
On days when she was absent,
With free periods all were blest,
Out of all the memories I've lived,
The classroom's are the best.
~Krish Kheskani

11. College Crush

Met her at the college gate,
Is this my fate?
I hope it works out,
Before it's too late.
I'd give her a ten,
If I were to rate,
I could give her time,
Even if there is lot on my plate.
Is she just a friend?
Or more than a batchmate,
If she finds me cute,
I shall celebrate.
Wanna know her past,
Wanna know her current state,
Could I be her future?
I don't know if we'll date,
Wonder what she loves,
Also, what she'll hate.
-Krish Kheskani

12. Mystery Girl

Just can't recall why,
That day I was so furious,
Your vibes pleased me,
Leaving me so curious.
Your alluring long hair,
Fair and rosy cheeks,
Gorgeous expressive eyes,
Radiant smile when you speak.
You're like an angel in uniform,
Wonder how you'd look in a dress,
I act so lame when you're around,
My first impression was a mess.
When you're around,
I can't stop to glance,
I look at you always,
When I get a chance,
You set the floor on fire,
With your dazzling dance.
The gentle tone you spoke,
Left me feeling pleased,
Your countenance was amiable,
And my anger now ceased.
Your accent was so different,

I wonder which state you belong,
Those headphones with you,
I wonder played which song.
I wonder what you dislike,
And what you like to eat,
So I could decide what to offer,
Spicy, salty, or sweet.
I wonder what clothes you like,
And what your fav colour was,
Wish I knew what's your ideal guy,
And know your strengths and flaws.
I wonder what your hobbies are,
And what are your life goals,
What you aspire to do,
And do you believe in souls.
Your one-minute presence,
Has cast a forever spell,
I cure faster thinking of you,
When I'm stressed and unwell.
I see you with open eyes,
I also see you when they're closed,
I visualise me with you,
Kneeling with a rose.
I see you in my dreams,
I think of you when I'm awake,
For us to be together,
Any risk I can take.

I feel I'm on seventh heaven,

Whenever you touch my hand,

I want us to laugh together,

Walking on golden sand.

If I could hold you in my arms,

My life would feel complete,

Not your body, it's your soul,

That swept me off my feet.

Be my life companion,

I ain't ever gonna cheat,

When you say good bye to leave,

I already miss you and wanna meet.

I wanna be your comb,

Running my fingers through your hair,

I wanna see it untied flying,

Kissing the windy air.

When we're together,

Our souls intertwine,

I'll be yours forever,

Just promise you'll be mine.

~Krish Kheskani

13. Principal Ma'am's Farewell

14. School Farewell

In playschool it started,
This journey of 13 years,
Entered the gates grumbling,
And now leaving with joyful tears.
This journey has evolved me,
Helping me overcome fears,
Never ever I realised that,
I would get so attached with peers.
I've learnt many subjects,
Like physics laws and English preposition,
I learnt values and manners,
Following the school tradition.
I recall how in first period,
The bell rang in the morning,
The same sound at the end of lunch,
Was more like a warning.
I'll always miss events,
Like annual day and elocution,
For such wonderful opportunities,
I thank this prestigious institution.
Football matches, school trips,
And the annual sports meet,
All these important days,

Have memories old and sweet.
I'll miss the ground,
Where we played football,
And how we judged assemblies,
Sitting in that hall.
The benches of the class,
The seats of the bus,
Even the staircase,
Holds a memory with us.
Though sometimes school mates fight,
There is never room for hate,
I have memories with all of them,
I love my every school mate.
For school, there is always,
A feeling of strong affection,
With every batchmate,
Feels a homely connection.
We must leave this second home,
Just like matured birds leave the nest,
This was just the first stage of life,
Life has more things to test.
The uniform has been like our skin,
The school logo is on our heart,
Yes, I'm leaving you my lovely school,
But my warmth for you will never part.
~Krish Kheskani

15. Sipping coffee at the window

Woke up very early this morning,

Saw dark circles under my eyes,

Made myself a coffee,

Well before the sunrise.

As I poured it into the cup,

I left the empty utensil behind,

If negativity could be poured out similarly,

All humans would have a healthy mind.

I sat at the window,

Staring at the lush green trees,

In the next moment I was mesmerized,

By the gentle rain and cool breeze.

I burnt my lips a little,

Trying to rapidly drink from the hot cup,

Just like my hasty moves in life,

Made my friendships messed up.

I looked down at the road,

Noticed puddles the rain had brought,

Just like they were filled with water,

My mind was filled with thought.

Reminiscing about some good days,

Regretting about the past,

Reminding myself it can't happen,
Recalling how things changed fast.
Wondering if it would be different,
If I told her earlier or later,
Or what if I hid it forever,
Would things then be better?
Does she think about me? Did my actions cost me a friend?
Will we ever make amends?
Lovers or friends happen, if meant,
Guess I should have no reason to repent.
Forgot about my cup while pondering,
I realised now my coffee was too cold,
You can't be too early or too late in life,
Right timing is worthier than gold.
Start living in the moment,
Be aware of what is right to do and say,
So you can have health, wealth and fruitful relations,
Don`t let your coffee get wasted at any day.
-Krish Kheskani

16. Expectations

So many expectations,
All born in the mind,
One wrong prediction,
Makes me feel blind.
Expected her to keep a secret,
Now it's heard by hundred ears,
Expected they'll make me smile,
All I got were tears.
Expected to win that medal,
Probably wasn't my day,
Life is an unfair game,
Sometimes tough to play.
Expected a quick reply,
My text wasn't ever seen,
Thought she was busy,
Her post popped my screen.
Expected her to text first,
Soon realised it's impossible,
Believed bonds can rebuild,
But egoism is so horrible.
Expected you to smile back,
But you turned away,
Thought you would listen,

All you do is say.
Expected you to make efforts,
Always I make the move,
Expected little trust,
Some feelings I can't prove.
Expected you to stay by my side,
When the world had torn me apart,
You just disappeared away,
Breaking my tender heart.
Expected you to apologise,
For stabbing my trust,
Expected you to give some time,
Can't your schedules adjust?
Expected some kindness,
For the massive love I gave,
Wish I never loved you,
I've dug my own grave.
Expected you to say 'Yes',
Learnt that won't happen ever,
You pushed me out of your life,
I've lost you forever.
Expected you to at least talk,
You just always ignore,
Expected you to never change,
Wish you were like before.
Expectation causes sorrow,
Gives me a heartache,

Stop expecting anything,
Then the world won't seem fake.
~Krish Kheskani

17. Deceptive First Impression

He comes wearing a trendy hat,
Seems a care free spoilt brat,
Well-dressed walked like a Chad,
Confidently with his friends he sat.
Clean shaved face, thick wavy hair,
Lean, tall, and slightly fair,
Seems a charming funny guy,
Jolly, frank and never shy.
Probably a party freak,
Last bencher, not a geek,
Goes places, meets people, spends money,
Can't be serious, always acts funny.
Social and makes great conversation,
Opens up without hesitation,
Gets too friendly, often does overshare,
Unknowingly creeps introverts out there.
Never tensed, he always smiled,
Walks and jumps while talking like a child,
They assumed he was an immature guy,
Sometimes first impressions are a lie.
Underneath this surface of immaturity,
Was a person with grace and dignity,

Street smart and responsible,
When needed, respectful and sensible.
Knows to tackle sensitive situations,
Thinks with calmness and patience,
Behind his dumb face, is a one very wise,
Who can help and give great advice.
His past experiences made him tough,
For his age, he knew more than enough,
Knew the kind he shouldn't trust,
Had vision to see beyond the dust.
Inquisitive of his father's occupation,
Works with him during vacation,
Does household chores for his mother,
Is an idol and advisor for his brother.
Aware of the world and people's nature,
Ambitious about his career and future,
Now they know him better so they imply,
His first impression was a lie.
-Krish Kheskani

18. God and Devil

If there is God,
Then there is also Devil,
Not every spirit is good,
Some are also evil.
The virtuous voice whispered,
While the wicked one screams,
I feel so puzzled,
They're often in my dreams.
The supreme suggests sympathy,
The devil demands destruction,
Punishment or forgiveness?
Which is the right instruction?
Steal, kill and betray,
The words of the cruel,
Do I have to pick a voice?
Can't I play it dual?
Usually I am loving,
But sometimes I make them whine,
Raised my arm and voice for myself,
Knowingly upset the divine.
The devil is black,
The God is white,
Humans are so grey,

There is no wrong or right.
Often the inner devil persuades,
To harm yourself or others,
To break free of those principles,
And that rule which smothers.
If you ask "God or Devil?"
I'll always say both,
Humans are fickle,
We don't follow our own oath.
We're a mixture of both,
We can't always stay serene,
We resemble none of them,
We're somewhere in between.
-Krish Kheskani

19. He wants to be heard

His unspoken words stifle him all week,
Sometimes he just wants to speak,
Willing to dig out each buried word,
Sometimes he just wants to be heard.
His sealed smiling lips lit up his cheek,
Ensuring he doesn't look weak,
He wants to tell how it occurred,
He just really wants to be heard.
Dares to speak what he never could,
Mind says "No" but heart feels he should,
Setting his caged feelings free as a bird,
Today he wants to be heard.
Though aloof from the herd,
He is not at all deterred,
To others, he might sound absurd,
He really wants to be heard.
His problems that often recurred,
The misery of the losses he incurred,
The horror of being least preferred,
He really wants to be heard.
-Krish Kheskani

20. Bird with a broken wing

The sky was clear,
Sun looked bright,
The injured one was left behind,
While the others took flight.
None of them waited back,
It shrieked all alone,
It's fellow mates abandoned him,
It's chirping was full of moan.
The other birds chirped merrily,
They all flew and sang along,
The injured one felt cold,
It wouldn't survive for long.
The other birds devoured worms,
The injured one just starved,
It's wing was broken,
And it's heart was also carved.
It kept longing to be with them,
It wanted to fly off the roof,
Though it was once one of them,
It's injury made him aloof.
It slowly started to realise,
It can't fly with them anymore,

His injury has changed everything,
It's wing and heart were sore.
~Krish Kheskani

21. The Shy Guy

He looks into the mirror,
Adjusting his nerdy glasses,
Just talks to himself all the time,
He is shy around the masses.
All guys around him are bulky,
He is thin and small,
Wonders why he can't gain,
Keeps wishing he was tall.
He is jittery and shaky,
He stammers a lot,
Fails to express and say,
The things that he had thought.
Around the girls he says nothing,
Doesn't utter a word,
The moment he tries to do so,
He ends up being absurd.
Unable to think of topics,
He fails to start a chat,
Fears to say certain things,
As people might judge that.
Unlike the sturdy confident guys,
He wasn't bold and loud,
Had he been more confident of himself,

He'd be loved by the crowd.
~Krish Kheskani

22. Overthinking

That day was years ago,
Still reflecting if it could be better,
Thinking of what's already done,
Wishing to change it later.
Mind overloaded with questions,
What if I didn't say that word?
What if I used another one?
Would it sound absurd?
Pondering about situations,
Evaluating my every fault,
Dwelling on how things could've been,
This mind just can't halt.
Asking and doubting myself,
Trying too hard for more precision,
Worrying about consequences,
Unable to make a decision.
Musing if I should blame myself,
Speculating if I'm cursed,
Out of all the people around,
My experiences are the worst.
Questions got into the head,
Was that too weird to wear?
Did I act too shy?

Did I overshare?
Confused whether to make amends,
Or just hold that grudge,
Analysing if I should trust,
Hoping they don't judge.
Making changes might help,
Like sharing less, listening more,
Is it worth to change your nature?
To just fit in with those four.
Feel and stay in the moment,
Don't misinterpret what they said,
Life is not at all complicated,
It's just a perspective in your head.
~Krish Kheskani

23. A part of me

A part of me wants to get serious,
Another part of me is just hilarious,
A part of me wants to shout in the crowd,
Another part of me is never ever loud.
A part of me wants to have fun,
"Leave these habits", said the other one,
A part of me wants to ring like an alarm,
The other one wanna stay calm.
A part of me wants to ignore the society,
This thought gives the other one anxiety,
A part of me has moved on from the past,
Sometimes the other one rewinds too fast.
A part of me wants to wait,
The other one thinks its late,
A part of me thinks like a kid,
The other one overthinks of what he did.
A part of me wants commitment,
The other one fears resentment,
A part of me wants attention,
The other one senses pretension.
A part of me wants a friend along,
The other one feels, alone is strong,
A part of me wants to mingle and goof,

The other one wants to stay aloof.

-Krish Kheskani

24. To my younger self

It's okay to feel this way,
It's alright to have a bad day,
Don't overanaylse what they said,
Don't let it stay in your head.
Express it to them, say it out loud,
Stop faking it to fit in the crowd,
Confide in someone you trust,
Letting out that feeling is a must.
The younger me said "they will judge",
This little boy wouldn't ever budge,
He was so used to suppress,
He was ignorant of how to express.
This suppression creates a bubble,
Bursting of which causes trouble,
You don't respond, you just react,
Impulsive decisions ruin your act.
Wish the younger me was wise,
Wish he knew a way to apologise,
Had he let more of himself shown,
His friendships would have grown.
Don't live beyond your means,
To blend in with silly teens,
If there is a need to chase,

True friendship wouldn't find place.
Wish he had better communication,
At any time, he could make conversation,
If he was confident of his every word,
Around any girl he wouldn't be awkward.
Life teaches at every stage,
Wisdom always grows with age,
Experience is like wine,
It takes time to become fine.
~Krish Kheskani

25. Is there something wrong?

It's okay to feel this way,
It's alright to have a bad day,
Don't overanaylse what they said,
Don't let it stay in your head.
Express it to them, say it out loud,
Stop faking it to fit in the crowd,
Confide in someone you trust,
Letting out that feeling is a must.
The younger me said "they will judge",
This little boy wouldn't ever budge,
He was so used to suppress,
He was ignorant of how to express.
This suppression creates a bubble,
Bursting of which causes trouble,
You don't respond, you just react,
Impulsive decisions ruin your act.
Wish the younger me was wise,
Wish he knew a way to apologise,
Had he let more of himself shown,
His friendships would have grown.
Don't live beyond your means,
To blend in with silly teens,

If there is a need to chase,
True friendship wouldn't find place.
Wish he had better communication,
At any time, he could make conversation,
If he was confident of his every word,
Around any girl he wouldn't be awkward.
Life teaches at every stage,
Wisdom always grows with age,
Experience is like wine,
It takes time to become fine.
~Krish Kheskani

26. That's not what I meant

27. Indecisive

Who am I?
What do I wanna be?
Should I cage myself,
Or shall I be set free?
Some days I want to dance,
Some days I want to sing,
Should I practice what I know?
Or pick up a new thing?
Should I buy those shoes?
Should I learn that skill?
Would it be worth?
Maybe it's just a thrill.
Am I good enough?
Probably can be better,
Is this the right time,
To send across that letter?
Do I really need someone?
Am I better alone?
Should I speak out loud?
Maybe I suit the lower tone.
Is it time to be serious?
Is it okay to be immature?
I have two extreme sides,

As I'm still not sure.

~Krish Kheskani

28. He was alone

He felt so lonely,
Around a buzzing crowd,
Only he was silent,
While others were loud.
He was aloof,
While others gathered,
Everyone was happy,
But he was shattered.
People enjoyed their time,
Held a celebration,
He was in a weird phase,
Full of desolation.
~Krish Kheskani

29. Time – The best healer

Bonds break because of ego,
There is no wrong or right,
The one who can't lose you,
Apologises to end the fight.
Impulsively people walk away,
For years they drift apart,
Their hearts often miss each other,
The ego wins over the heart.
One day the heart speaks out,
Finally, they realise,
They regret holding on,
Wishing they'd been wise.
Not all have such courage,
Some rejected what the heart brought,
They still live merry lives,
As they moved on and forgot.
It takes years to build trust,
Barely seconds to break,
In the journey of healing,
You decide the time you take.
All take some time to heal,
Maybe a week or years,
When you learn to "not hold on",

You'll never be left in tears.
Sun once set takes time to rise,
"Your sun shall rise ",
Once told by a great man,
I realise he was wise.
True bonds turn stronger than ever,
Once they start to heal,
Weak ones heal partially,
Failing to give that feel.
True bonds are like a thread,
Their healing is a knot,
This knot doesn't let it break,
But it won't be the same like you thought.
~Krish Kheskani

30. A Divine End (Witnessing death)

His legs lost all strength,
His hands got all numb,
I tried to talk to him,
But he just kept mum.
I moved towards him,
Held and felt his hand was cold,
His mouth wasn't shut,
Unconscious open eyes so bold.
He calmly laid down in bed,
His face turned pale,
Body felt heavier,
It was the end of his tale.
It marked the end of suffering,
He was now free of pain,
Found the divine peace,
Which the alive can't gain.
This end is a new beginning,
For his fortunate next life on earth,
The gentle soul being immortal,
Finds a new body for the next birth.
Be kind to everyone,
Do it on all days,

So you don't regret it,
When they part ways.
~Krish Kheskani

31. The Lost Boy

Everyone found him too weird,
He had a half-grown beard,
There was a lot he never expressed,
Everyone thought he was depressed.
The close ones knew his problem,
They could read his face,
He never actually meant,
Whatever he says.
He sometimes wished to socialise,
But often liked to be alone,
He had feelings in his heart,
Which he had barely shown.
He saw things differently,
He probably overthought,
He questioned why can't he be different,
It's answer he never got.
He stopped expressing himself,
As he feared all would judge,
He suddenly felt to ignore the world,
Now even his close ones hold a grudge.
Soon something struck his mind,
The lost boy found his path one day,
He realised his passions and dreams,

When he kept the world away.
He was no more frowning,
He became courteous and amiable,
No one ever thought,
The lost boy could be affable.
Now his city loves him,
His people want him back,
He became a perfect guy,
After finding all he lacked.
~Krish Kheskani

32. Dear God, Is this love ?

God let me cherish this forever,
Don't let this moment end,
Could you please stop the time,
Or let me earn it back like money spent.
Though change is the only constant,
I hope few bonds stay the same,
I feel like I already know her,
Even though I just heard her name.
People can hurt you,
Staying cautious is a must,
Some may feel it's too early,
But my heart tells me to trust.
I hope this vibe escalates,
So we know each other better,
God, I know you want the best for me,
So I am writing you this letter.
I hope this spark is forever,
None of us gets bored of the other,
I hope there is good communication,
So none of us ghosts the other.
I hope for healthy discussions of issues,
Rather than fights and ignorance,
I hope our conversation never dies,

We boost each other's confidence.
You often feel attraction,
But seldom feel a connection,
Wish every misunderstanding dies,
With you around, my time flies.
So engaged in our conversation,
Can't even watch cricket on television,
As soon as I look at you,
Everything else goes out of vision.
Let me adore you, just stand by,
I miss you after every good bye,
I'd tell you we're just friends,
But to you, I can never lie.
-Krish Kheskani

33. On seventh heaven

You've proven everyone wrong,
You've got all the attention,
You're on seventh heaven,
Will this last? To yourself you question.
You've received admiration,
Strikingly fast like thunder,
You're on seventh heaven,
Will it fade faster? You wonder.
~Krish Kheskani

34. Is it wrong to feel this?

Is it wrong to feel this?
Is there a way to heal this?
It's now like a curse,
Which first felt like a bliss.
Is it wrong to feel this?
Those moments now I don't miss,
What earlier felt almighty,
Now gives me anxiety.
Is it wrong to feel this?
Those moments I don't reminisce,
Someone else makes me smile,
Giving butterflies once a while.
Is it wrong to feel this?
These feelings I can't dismiss,
This phase is draining and dark,
I'm looking for a new spark.
-Krish Kheskani

35. Should you let it out?

Should you let it out?
Or let it stay for a while,
Should you express grief?
Maybe hide it with a smile.
Should you let it out?
That feeling of affection,
Or maybe lie to yourself,
Denying it as silly attraction.
Should you let it out?
The innocence of your mind,
Or continue fearing,
That they'll stop being kind.
Should you let it out?
The horror of losing someone close,
Or just let things be,
So the bond still grows.
-Krish Kheskani

36. Is there more to it?

Is this just a phase?
It ain't found at every place,
Is there more to it?
Or is it destined to replace?
Is this just momentary?
Maybe little more than temporary,
Is there more to it?
Let fate decide this worry.
Some may say its casual,
But it's different than the usual,
Is there more to it?
Am I being delusional?
Is this out of boredom?
I know this phase is random,
Is there more to it?
It feels more than just a tantrum.
Is this a true connection?
God give me more conviction,
Is there more to it?
Help me see through this reflection.
Is it okay to trust?
The spark is beyond silly lust,
Is there more to it?

God let me know what I must.
Are these just few common beliefs?
Are we just our griefs' reliefs,
I think there is more to it,
Just a co-incidence is hard to believe.
-Krish Kheskani

37. I miss you

I miss those endless talks,
The unplanned long walks,
The random late-night call,
And together playing football.
When your fav song is played,
Your image gets portrayed,
Mind goes on a flashback mode,
Your memories are a precious load.
Reading your name, I turn blind,
Your voice pops up my mind,
Your gentle smile and face,
I wish to see always.
Those days when you teased me,
They really pleased me,
I've looked in every place,
But old relations can't replace.
I remember your fav player and team,
Even your preferred ice cream,
My persuasions when you got pissed,
All of you has been missed.
I remember your silly joke,
And all those things you spoke,
Your lovely pretty eyes,

Which caught in mine, my naughty lies.

The soothing look you gave me,

Left me in full of glee,

In college, students were plenty,

But without you class felt empty.

The lovely places we went,

That gala time we spent,

All has now become history,

Life seems like a mystery.

In a crowded party with buzzing sound,

I miss you and want you around,

With the tastiest food and finest beer,

All I say "Wish you were here".

Why do you turn your face away,

Please listen to what I gotta say,

Stop acting that I don't exist,

Trust me dear you've been missed.

This time don't turn away,

"Come back", I often pray,

If you do, I must say,

"Don't leave again, always stay. "

~Krish Kheskani

38. You're cringy

Today you call me cringy,
Before I was your pride,
My soul's waves are rising in misery,
Because of your high tide.
For you, I kept my work aside,
Every weekend we met,
"You're so cringy man",
That is all I get?
I used to call you daily,
Before going to bed,
"You're really cringy",
That is what you said.
You used to like my shoes,
Loved my shirt in red,
"The way you dress is cringy",
Yes, I heard what you said.
The shows we watched together,
And all the books we have read,
"All your choices are cringy",
That is what your said.
You're always busy now,
It feels like you're dead,
Since now I am cringy,

You hang out with others instead.
For the way I look, talk, and joke,
And all the posts in my feed,
You call me cringy for who I am,
So yes, I'm cringy indeed.
~Krish Kheskani

39. Lies

Are you lying to her?
Is she lying to you?
You're both lying to yourself,
Do you have any clue?
You'll be lost in her,
When she is lost in him,
Yes, she was your sunshine,
But you can't always stay dim.

-Krish Kheskani

40. Mesmerised

When I saw you in that outfit,
You were bit overdressed,
I swear I was no more depressed,
Instead, I felt delighted,
My feelings unexpressed,
I know I looked weird,
My face was little stressed.
You did great,
I was the one who messed,
I think about it now and then,
I feel I am obsessed.
Having met you I feel blessed.
~Krish Kheskani

41. If we could turn back time

I wish some things were same again,
Just like the way before,
It's tough to believe,
They can't change anymore.
I wish we could talk again,
And I could make you smile,
But we haven't seen each other,
It's now been a while.
Wish you trusted me,
And were still the same,
Don't know if you even,
Remember my name.
Let's just own up for mistakes,
And accept we were wrong,
Apart we are quite good,
But together we stand strong.
~Krish Kheskani

42. Present Feels Right

• 75 •

Clear minds on a blurry night,
The dark sky, our mood so bright,
Ignoring worries, feeling light,
Don't emphasize future, present feels right.

Quotes

"Work is a boon that keeps your mind busy"

"Even the finest artists in the world have critics. What makes you think people should appreciate you? Self-validation is the key to everything."

"Any sort of bond or socializing is toxic if you have to play mind games."

"Receiving and reciprocating affection is always less hurtful than initiating. As you're unaware of the consequence it takes more courage to express. It's better to stay at the receiving end if you know you're vulnerable."

"Friendships and relationships are like the sky above your head. The sky represents the weather. The people you chose to keep around impact your life's weather. Staying with the right ones brings out the best weather."

"Stories of your life will never be perfect, if they were then they wouldn't be worth telling."

"Just if one flower loses it's fragrance doesn't mean that all in the bouquet are odourless. There is surely a fragrant one which you will love but you must give yourself a chance to find out. Don't let bad experiences prevent you from your deserved flower"

"You will always feel you gave more than you got till you realise what you can be grateful for."

"Life is like a thread. Our past mistakes are like a tight knot which cannot be untied. Similarly, mistakes can be ignored but not be forgotten."

"There is never a right moment express something. The moment you do, makes it the right one."

"If they do not respond to your plans, opinions, and thoughts with the same energy. Then stop bothering them and move on."

"All those frowning feelingless faces are the ones longing for most affection."

"Life is like a book, but pages can be turned back, time cannot. Reading previous pages can be helpful to interpret but don't engross yourself so much that you forget which page were you actually on."

"Failure is better than a missed opportunity."

"Money can't buy love, friendship, happiness, health and respect."

"Some people will never forgive you, in that case you need to forgive yourself and move on. Not you, they are the ones holding on to the emotional baggage of the past."

"It takes a big heart to apologise but it takes a bigger one to forgive and give another chance."

"If you forgive but change your behaviour towards them means you never really forgave them."

Poetry And People's Minds

An irrational mind criticizes poetry,
    An immature mind jokes about it,
    An emotional mind understands it,
    An honourable mind respects it,
    An innovative mind reads it,
    A creative mind creates it.

-Krish Kheskani

A Conversation With God

Is it insane to still regret and whine over the decisions you made years back? Is it wrong to wonder how things could have turned out?

What if your life didn't turn around? There were many upsides to this rough turn but it still stabs my heart thinking that why did it have to end this way? Why does a new beginning need an end? Why can't I hold on to that past moment and cherish the present too?

This tiny feeling is like a pinch which runs down my spine every now and then. It's a phase where I dive into and ocean of nostalgia which is so deep that I can't reach the surface in a single breath so I keep diving into it every now and then. This phase mostly occurs to people when they're about to sleep.

It's like a catchy jingle which gets triggered every time I observe the slightest vision or sound providing enough evidence to recall the lines leading me to sing it in it's very catch tune.

Is this a boon or a bane?

Will there be a remedy?

Till when will I continue hearing this melody?